DOWSING

poetry by

Georgia Santa Maria

© 2017 Georgia Santa Maria

All rights reserved. No part of this book may be reproduced without the express written permission of the author, except in the case of written reviews.

ISBN 978-1-929878-63-5

First edition

PO Box 5301
San Pedro, CA 90733
www.lummoxpress.com

Printed in the United States of America

Dedicated to my sons
Nicky, Chris and Nathan
and
the New Mexico Poetry Community

Acknowledgments

City Blues won 1st Place in Alibi, the 10th Anniversary of 9-11 Issue, published 9/11/2011, also appearing in Lichen Kisses, pub. 2014.

Drought was published in LUMMOX #5, 2016 and was First Runner-up in the LUMMOX Poetry Contest.

Apology to My Husband was also published in LUMMOX #5, 2016.

Instant was published in Duke City Fix, The Sunday Poem, 10/09/16.

Revolution was published in LUMMOX #5, 2016.

Suitcase was published in Fixed and Free Poetry Anthology, 2015

Ten Penny Nails won the National Federation of State Poetry Societies, 2nd Prize, 2014 It was published in Encore Anthology, 2015

The Vegan Feminist Dilemma was published in Adobe Walls Anthology, 2014.

Women on the Money was published by LUMMOX #5 2016

About This Book

This volume of poetry is the prize for winning the 3rd LUMMOX Poetry Prize by default. Each year, the LUMMOX Poetry Anthology runs a poetry contest...the winning prize includes 40 copies of a special chapbook of the winner's work, a feature in the anthology and a small cash prize.

6 • Are The Bees Awake Yet?
8 • Blackbirds
9 • The Hot Cossack
10 • City Blues
11 • Dowser
12 • Drought
14 • Escaping Woman
15 • Apology to My Husband
16 • Geographic
17 • Hollyhocks
18 • Horses
20 • Imaginary Italy
22 • On Studying an Infrared Photo of My Home
23 • Instant
24 • "It didn't taste the way it used to taste to me."
25 • Meadowlark
26 • Landfill Versus Dump
28 • Manzano
30 • Revolution
32 • Russian River
33 • Suitcase
34 • Sunflower Castle
35 • The Tea Cup
36 • Ten Penny Nails
37 • The Vegan Feminist Dilemma
38 • on the Money
40 • Wind
41 • About the Author

Are The Bees Awake Yet?
Placitas, NM March 12, 2016

Somebody should tell
the blossoms to slow-down.
Too early—anxious as
adolescents to grow,
blooming shadowed by snow.
The precarious Santa Fe apricots,
wild plums that grow along the ditch
of a mountain village,
before Lent is done, before
the ditch's communal cleaning,
before the water gets turned on.
Snow-flake blossoms against
the black of winter branching,
the brackish leaves of the previous fall.
The pink of promised peaches,
like Easter's little girls,
have come too soon.
The clouds gather grey and
black along the mountain.

Looking north, we see new snows.
The wind gusts encircle the valley
and Jemez disappears.
We dilute our hope with our foreboding:
we've seen this too many times before.
The apricots make one year out of seven,
we're overdue a freeze this year.
A friend strings Christmas lights
among the branches—it seems to work,
a saving miracle. She's had apricots
the last two years in a row;
a serious cause for optimism.
The memory of their sweetness
and their golden color, miracles,
a way of saying we're forgiven
out of sun and rain and blossoms,
and prayer.

Blackbirds

I've always loved the black and white,
shades of grey: old car tires, striated
against their cousin highways paved.
Linoleum blocks, printed
photographs before the '60s:
Margaret Bourke White
and Dianne Arbus
cut to the chase.
A partial appeal of this ink,
this pen. The simplicity of a pencil
on good paper, thick as cream.
Trace the nude figure, plaintive
abandoned trailer and its weeds,
grasses bending in a spiral wind.
A complexity of snowfall,
flying punctuation against a stormy sky
that's always moving, rumbling
threats and unkept promises for rain,
a perpetual grey surprise
that leaves a blue day boring.
The subtlety of *bosque* winters,
layered grasses where birds can hide,
until a screen-door slams,
and then, an explosion,
a firework of blackbirds taking flight.

The Hot Cossack

I had an erotic dream, once, about Leonid Brezhnev.
He was hot, and sweet to me. I was so in love.
Scorch-marked!
I awoke baffled, never having thought of
any Soviet leader in that way. Though,
I suppose they DO. Mother Russia's
populated most of a continent.
But, Leonid Brezhnev?
With his fur hat and overcoat?
I dreamed he was naked underneath,
and Hairy, like a big pink bear.
I liked it. Liked him. Couldn't get enough:
his tallow scent, his huffle-grunts,
the luscious, lascivious, lusting Premier.
I was his secret darling,
in a dark grey room with dirty sheets.
What does it mean?
What does it mean?
I felt a pang of sadness when he died,
for lost opportunity. But why?
Sometimes, you just have to wonder
where <u>that</u> came from, amongst
a universe of possibilities.

City Blues

Into the great blue lonely
cold morning, the sun hidden
but for a *moue* on the clouds.
In the gutter, a cigarette
rides along, buoyed by
a crushed lipstick print.
The attempted lift, a weight
of sorrow, of exhaustion.
Through the cold, the sun
attempts to rise
above the mountain,
to light the concrete,
dry the morning sidewalks.
Call the street sweeper
to prepare the day for
civilized souls and business,
all the comings and goings
of wingtips and high heels
and elevator rides up to nowhere.

Dowser

Arnold Sturdy dowsed for water
taught me "dig here"
where the green sticks cross over.
Underground, streams
cross shelves of shale.
Dig the well, and you'll hear the trickle.
Now, they tilt in, from over a mile,
after natural gas and shale-oil,
frack, like desultory teenagers
with slumping backs, careless
of our need for a clean cold drink,
for either a man or his livestock tank.
The weary water, muddied and poisonous,
I wonder if Arnold's green twigs would still cross.

Drought

This drought
an invitation to decendance
noticeable only by increments--
blades of grass diminishing,
the paucity of tepid squalor.
Hope
continuing, intermittent,
and rare as rain.
A cursive snail's trail of water lawyers
protecting wealthy clients.
Still--
the wood on old barn sides
logs the insults of the wind.
Whorls and spirals spinning,
a mirror in the wood
tells everything.
The orchard stumps remembering
the juiciness of apples held aloft,
birds singing.
Even the magpie can't find
anything left to steal.

The licoriced clouds
that used to carry rain
have drowned
and left a dust-cloud,
just as black.
It takes, instead of giving,
obscures the mountain
and the sun, and
lonesome cows, gathered
beside the last, lonely pond
stand, eyes to tail,
side to side
sheltering each other
from the sand.

Escaping Woman

Sailing her calyx into the wilderness,
in the heat of a mid-life swivel,
away with this and come to that,
a beach, a mountain, a river.
Anything but the languishing love,
anything with vibration,
sinuous as a garden hose,
the highway connects to everything.

She prays for the mysterious,
raveling around the corners
of canyons, and mesas, rising
like a Bollywood chorus,
sambas of sandstone, bluffing
redder than sunset,
bluer than Brahma,
white as God's wingtips.
The reversal of light
to sky and ground:
earth, ethereal and cloud white,
the sky thick and black as a bruise.

She clings to the current,
no long goodbyes to the garden,
destination a state of mind,
she thinks only of up—
ascending, like Icarus,
toward the sun.

Apology to My Husband

Instead of cleaning house
for your cousins' visit tomorrow,
today I wrote a poem.
I really loved the poem.
Loved writing it, and loved reading it.
Loading the dishwasher,
not so much, I admit.
The bathroom floor is full of dog-hair,
and the toilet has a pink ring around the bowl
like a Texaco station, neglected on Route 66.
And the chicken juice from the groceries last week
is still puddled up on the refrigerator's second shelf.
Your bed, which they're supposed to sleep in,
has the same sheets it had six months ago
and no blankets.
You share your bedroom with the dog.
I won't be cooking tomorrow, either. You'll
probably have to get something to take-out.
I haven't shopped since the leaky chicken—
y'all might need some eggs or bread or milk.
I'll see you later—I'm taking my poem
up to Santa Fe and reading it to my friends.
Tell your cousins I said "Hello, and Best Wishes,"
and that I wrote you a poem.

Geographic

The yellow of morning, whiskey.
The yellow of evening, gin.
Jaundice, the yellow eye,
a pontoon liver, cheek and chin—
A man signals his direst need,
a yellow flag in a yellow breeze.
The yellow of urine, of marigolds,
flowers of the dead.
The rain-soaked cliffs turn
the river, first yellow, then red.
A yellow sky, to complement
the mountains, purple as Lent.
The silhouette of a rider, heading west
toward that great horizon.
A yellow moon on an
always receding ocean:
How can it not come back again?
As if on stilts, he walks
on toothpick legs, a bird,
within sight of predatory animals.
A dispassionate clockwork waits
to record the inevitable yellow end.

Hollyhocks

I looked for you today
as I passed the road to Ojito,
the canyon a ridiculous occurrence:
they've white-washed Idy's rock house
and teenagers float south
in little rubber blue boats.

I looked for you
in my green burrito,
but my *sopapilla* hadn't risen
and was flat.

I looked for you
in the smell of rain,
insinuating itself
impotent and broken
above the mountain,
the color bruised.

I looked for you
in the bar, remembering
the night of Black Russians.
None of the hats were
bent just right.

I looked for you
in the hollyhocks of summer,
pink and red up against the wall
like dissidents in front of
a firing squad.

Horses

They spoke of the healing power of horses:
sad children brought into sync with
a calm Universe, slowed to the speed of grass,
the squeak of saddle leather, a huffel of breath,
steam from the magical beasts.
The dusty sweated hides glimmer of sunlight,
the child perched upon this fleshy mountain,
singing the music of the lungs.

A hundred years ago, a common thing,
integral to small traveling,
the horse as companion, in street or
barn or pasture, the ancient paddock
circumscribed by silvered wood.

We are old friends, people and horses—
a kind of broken separation intercedes:
they've gone wilder, we more civilized,
a memory in the DNA of time.
Nostalgia buys a movie screen.

Or else, the rarefied niche of winter cowboys,
clopping hooves, the body splits the wind.
Still hired to find lost calves in springtime
snowstorms: frozen faces, frozen hands
knitting-up the barb-wire to keep the cattle in.
A good hat won't blow off, keeps the rain
off your neck. Breathe in the melting snowflake,
think of the kindness of the line-shack,
and for them, a warm, dry, hay-filled shed.

And then, some warm Saturday morning
along a dirt trail, convergence once again,
the wild horses come, unexpected
to surprise us as half-forgotten dreams.

Imaginary Italy

In the dappling evening light, I'll go
to my imaginary Italy,
where Marcello pours me grappa,
and feeds me olives from his hillside trees,
the gold of sun on a summer wall
against the purpling evening.
I will bring paints and canvas
rolled up in my bag, (better than
extra sweaters, or heeled shoes.)
I will be barefoot all day.
A deep blue pool, behind a wall
will welcome me with its cold.
I shall float and dive, like a swallow in flight.
Thick stone will guard the room
where I sleep, an open window
lets in the cool night,
and the gauze of white curtains
will catch the moon light
and greet me as I'm waking.
I will drink espresso, bitter and black
in the plaza cafe, church bells will ring,
and lined-up children walk to school
in white sox and black shoes,
led by a nun. The one
at the end of the line dawdles,
stops to scratch an itchy shin,
then grins over to me.

He might be Marcello's son.
At night, I will rediscover the moon,
new words will come to my tongue,
filagreed and ornamental, sleek
and fast, like "Lamborghini."
I will drive the cliff's edge
looking out at the sea, in a car
like a roller-skate for the body.
Flirt with the grandfather
who plays the accordion
in the restaurant managed by his son.
These old Italian songs, finiculi-finicula,
taste like red sauce and history,
a people gifted in the art of fun,
gifted in love, and gifted in living.
I will find myself, as if painted
by Botticelli, floating on the sea.

On Studying an Infrared Photo of My Home:

An infrared satellite map shows water in red
like blood in the vein, across the earth
The irrigated field, a patch of vermillion,
next to its dry blue brother. This is
a map of intention, who's dry, who's wet
where the water flows by human interference,
as opposed to just some river-bed,
curving its own curly canyon, or arroyo
if there's not enough grass to hold the soil down.
There are no maps to show the wind,
except in its relationship to drying up the ground,
the dying of the trees, becoming pale as stones
the infrared measures life in terms of color,
heat and water, makes no judgments,
just shows it like it is. But on the ground,
looking up for rain, it is all the difference.

Instant

Seven sooty children,
tumbling over the dunes
and into the raucous sea.
The beach, windblown and
wild in grass and birdcalls,
drowned out by the boom
and crush of waves,
breaking on the beach.
These kids, fearless and feral
as gulls in the lifting breeze,
right now, belong to no one
but this ocean and this
instant in their being.

"It didn't taste the way it used to taste to me."
(Mary McGinnis)

The chutney, sugar-sweet, has lost its peppery tang.
The birthday cake, white and bland, reminiscent of flour and crisco—
where have all the sugary roses gone?
Broccoli, pungent, green and gassy, now wooden, needing salt.
The bitterness of coffee, morning's first sip—a good start.
Good stiff tea's tannins dry out the mouth.
Most, I miss the way he fried a chicken,
succulent as himself.

Meadowlark

Burned with listening
to this blighted language.
The languid purple blossom
in the background,
a locked landscape,
penetrating our lament.
Reminder of that other
reality: that of bees
and flowerings, their words
unkempt and riotous
along the wind--
like dust motes, soon
disappearing
beyond our ken,
or caring.
Inside the tree is hiding
the noisy meadowlark,
now quiet--contemplating
two pink translucent eggs
who will become
next summer's singing.

Landfill Versus Dump

A trip to the dump in the old days, pre-landfill,
not so self-aware, nor were we, scouting out
for beautiful detritus, new used living-room furniture,
a favorite table, wide for puzzles, edged so
the marbles won't roll off and get lost,
build a clay tableau of dinosaurs in their forests,
keep a corner for the mail, coupons and bills.
We comb the arroyos of other people's trash
like panthers, filled with fleshly lust for things,
canning jars and bottles, turned lavender in the sun.
Once I found a washing machine made of wood
with armature and paddles, made to roll and shake
to clean the clothes. It was pre-electric, magical
and sturdy, with a wringer mounted up above.
Miles and miles of bent-up barb-wire fencing,
and hog-wire, and chicken-wire—made me wonder
why anyone would go to a store to buy the stuff.
We fenced our entire pasture free of charge.
It took some time unbending the old kinks,
but all and all was pretty good. The telephone
co-op left bales of black-wrapped wire the kids used
to improve their fort and string-up the elevator Nicky built.

There was always tons of wood for kindling or repairing
funky board, chicken coops and barn-sides, some
tin roofing—fill the holes with silicon, and patch
my leaky studio and right up over the kids' bunks.
There's wire and posts for clotheslines, to go with
that old washer, and a modestly dented dishpan
to heat water in. Lots of household treasures.
All they need is a little cleaning and polishing,
zip-strip and bar-varnish heaven.
Once, there was a whole wood-stove!
Fred put it in his mother's kitchen. Nowadays,
the EPA declares open dumps a hazard, (though
they still allow underground fracking—which is
the rummaging around, equivalent of dump-picking,
after substrates of oil and gas, injecting poison
to keep them floating to the surface for collection.)
Now, everything else gets buried, usefulness or not —
cover it up with borrowed dirt, and a cluster of
suburban housing. Don't tell the new folks
to the neighborhood. Just wait till it starts decomposing,
and the water tastes like a 1954 Pontiac car hood.

Manzano

The rain's gift is color—
the periwinkle blue of distance,
a springtime chartreuse, against the rusted barn,
red as the Emperor's jacket,
red as the Pope's shoes.

The old spring-box flows white with watercress
above the lake, where the water is its cleanest.
I saw an ancient apricot, frosted this year,
blessed with leaves, but no fruit. The trunk
a twist of rope, merry with orange lichen.

A rattlesnake, undisturbed, hides between
fossiled layers of cool limestone,
out of the hot sun.

Mud-daubers, swallows, rush the puddle
brought by last night's rain storm—
a flutter of wings, they fill their beaks to build
their nests, under the Church's eaves.

Splashes of white droppings disturb
the symmetry of blue stained glass.
The interior Saints appearing
in the windows, distant and mysterious,
white shadows behind dark glass.

The poor carve natural headstones for their kin.
A *Campo Santo* reflects the village that it's in.
A plot with angels, ironwork, marbled glory next to
this warm flagstone, with a fading ancient name.
The rain has made flowers between all of them.

Iris, a purple show with long green stem,
multiplies into a knotty celebration,
mitered as a Bishop, poor as the farmers beneath them.

Revolution
> *For Grace Lee Boggs, June 27, 1915 – October 5, 2015*
> *Revolutionary Civil Rights Leader & Activist*

Revolution is not hard—
it is soft. Rolls in,
like the moon on the ocean,
and back out again.
Uses guitars, and paint brushes
more effectively than guns.
Changes minds and emotions
before the explosions
of blood and hatred.
Revolution lasts better
on a full stomach—
involves family recipes,
and new ingredients,
untasted flavors, and
the suspension of sameness
it takes to learn
to like something new.
The best soldiers are children:

babies teach patience
and how to soar by the
seat of your passion
and imagination.
The best revolutions
begin in the kitchen,
move to the den, with friends
and wind up in the bedroom:
most marvelous advice,
sleep on it.
A revolution should grow
at the speed of grass,
take hints from the wild flower,
who says,
"See—I'm not a weed!
Who else will feed
all these wild birds,
and make good use of bees."

Russian River

And finally the sea, the cliffs
these giant wind-bent cedars,
they hold the dark and frame
the white and blue of ocean.
Just past the Russian River,
where your own spawn
threw your ashes in,
like some poor lost salmon,
never to make it home again.
There was a sense of longing,
missing you, as if this wasn't
so beautiful a view.
This highway makes me
think of Steve McQueen,
a little sports car, built for two,
racing into blue oblivion
like you.

Suitcase

The eager rhapsody, barreling toward bliss,
a Dionysian station-wagon to the beach.
Wisteria heartbeat, lavender
washing-line in the breeze.
Springtime, you old suitcase
full of joy and half-kept promises,
blossomings and freezings,
the consummate joke of the season:
fifteen pink tulips
in a fifty mile-an-hour wind.
Such a sense of humor!
All the lilacs laugh—
such good drought-struck plants.
A weathering, constant and eternal,
the sandblasting of children's skin.
March comes in like a lion,
goes out like Joseph Stalin.

Sunflower Castle

Searching old photos for memory,
they look like illustrations
from some Fairy-Tale book:
exaggerated, a life so fantastical
I know it could not have been lived.
Surely I could not have done those things:
a house fit for dwarves, fields for fairies,
a Prince, now long dead,
with a face made of love
and a giant carrot from the garden
sticking out of his head.
Huge white geese as footmen
guard the crumbling castle,
precariously made from
toothpicks and bubblegum.
Who could have lived like that?

The Tea Cup

There is a place the potter missed.
A tear-drop gap within the glaze,
two hundred years of tea has stained
with the memories of other times--
an Emperor, before the Wars,
a pristine woods, a Samurai,
the lives of cranes beside a pond,
in conversation, then in flight.
Peonies like a young girl's cheek,
bamboo leaves, where life can hide,
the blue of heaven reflecting in
the line of water the clay invites.

Clay, fire and water make all three,
the potter, the teacup, and the tea.

Ten Penny Nails

In the hardware bin of nails and screws
bits of lint collect, mouse pellets fall
to the bottom, impossible to separate.
A gouging claw grabs a cactus of iron.
A few fall, hit the flooring tile,
sounding out the clink of their spill.
The thinness of the paper sack
mimics the thinness of my skin.
Nail ends, jammed in, poke through--
always too many on the scale, or too few.
Now, at places like Home Depot,
they sell them in a box, neat--
the perfect pound, down to the nail,
all facing North, like obedient soldiers.
Still, there was a beauty in
the spin of the bin, around--
like some prickly carousel,
full of dangerous choices.

The Vegan Feminist Dilemma

The contest calls for poetry from a "Vegan Feminist" perspective--
(a daily non-sequitur selection from the spin-cage of the web,)
the planetary revolve of possibilities. Might just as well have been
"Carnivorous Pederasts" or "The Omnivores Of Dominance,"
addressing the eating habits of sexual politics:
What do we eat in bed?
The obvious answer, of course: each other. Though that,
removed a pace from Global Warming, or PETA,
or Max Factor's testing labs. From the ranch-lands of Wyoming:
Can cowboys be feminists? Perhaps, an anthology called
"Feminists on Horseback." You want a banana with that?
Wyoming granted suffrage fifty years ahead of the US Congress,
Utah shortly after that. Neither state known for being Vegan,
or, these days, feminist. Does meat put hair on your chest?
Do bean-sprouts cause equal pay-checks?
Does celery help girls with their math?
Will there be fewer unwanted pregnancies if we eat more tofu?
Headline: " With The Aid Of Pineapple, The Glass Ceiling Was Cracked."
"Executive Credits Brown Rice With Promotion."
Confusing the contents of our stomachs with
the contents of our lives, our uteruses, and our heads:
Are six-inch spike heels any less vicious made of plastic?
Do we run faster wearing vinyl loafers?
Does it do a girl advantage to be foot-bound and emaciated?
Gives her a slim chance for fighting back, or climbing upward.
Why are we perpetually faced with idiotic choices, like:
"Should I eat, or just *become* a vegan tart?" and,
"What *am* I made of, but meat?"

Women on the Money

Eleanor Roosevelt had no chin.
Buck-toothed, and a little too fat.
Dowdy, even, besides
she was a pushy dame
always wanting this and that,
fairness, etcetera,
for workers, children and blacks.

And, while you might trust Rosa Parks,
to clean your house,
or raise your children,
why put her on the money, when
we didn't even want to pay her, much—
why do you think she was
riding the bus, anyway?
She didn't even own a Cadillac.

As for Sacajawea,
we already went there once,
with those pretty little gold dollars
that flopped. Except for
birthday presents for the kids
and gathering dust in coin collections.
That should be a hint.

Carrie Nation got us prohibition.
What an idiot idea was that?
Clara Barton was a pretty good nurse,
and nobody minded her beside their bed.
But a nurse?
And not a doctor?
What's with that?

Dolly Madison threw great parties,
and her name's still on the pastries.
While John Adams was away in Paris,
Abigail took good care of the kids,
and wrote some awesome letters.
I suppose they were both pretty nice girls.

Hillary might well become our first woman President,
because she has that "Clinton Dynasty" behind her,
and she went to Yale when it was nearly still all men,
which is impressive. But, do we want
someone who's always wearing pant-suits?
And she wasn't willing to throw her husband out for cheating,
or under Ken Starr's bus. Though,
God knows, it was her fault that he cheated,
for being such a frigid witch.
I heard she threw a lamp!
Do we really want somebody who can't
control her temper?
Or her hairdo?
Or Bill's dick?

Let's put Marilyn on the money!
She already has a marvelously successful stamp!
God knows, she was the epitome of pretty!
Had great tits.
Had the grace to die young, before getting lumpy.
And was glamorous enough to date presidents.
We use her image to decorate all those "retro" diners
coast to coast. She was blonde,
and didn't venture an opinion anyone can remember.
And, just knowing she's in your pants
will make you want to carry tens.

Wind

This clinquant wind, shimmering
its way through leaky windows
wavy with age
the light across the sill, the light
through a lace curtain,
dancing flowers on the floor
across my hand, across the wall.
A whispering first, in the morning,
a roaring in the afternoon.
In the treetops above the roof,
the clattering of loose tin
glinting in sun, or moonlight,
a resistance rusted and torn,
sharp against the rounded wind,
cut and cutting, then giving in.

Georgia Santa Maria is a Native New Mexican, and has been an artist, photographer, and writer most of her life. She has been published in many anthologies and other local and national publications. In 2012 she was a Guest Editor for LUMMOX Poetry Anthology, Issue I. Her book of poetry and photographs, Lichen Kisses was published in April, 2013. In the summer of 2014 she traveled to Germany, where she was a featured reader in Berlin. She is currently working on another poetry book, a cookbook, and a book of short stories. Her work may be found online at Duke City Dime Stories: the 'best of' collection. Recently, she was first runner-up for the LUMMOX 5 Poetry Prize, featured in the current issue of LUMMOX Poetry Anthology #5.

The LUMMOX Press was established in 1993
and has published the Little Red Book series,
the LUMMOX Journal, and publishes chapbooks,
a perfect bound book series (the Respect series),
a Poetry Anthology & Poetry Contest (annually),
and "e-copies" (PDFs) of all it's books.

The goal of the press and its publisher is to
elevate the bar for poetry, whilst bringing
the "word" to an international audience.
We are proud to offer this book
as part of that effort.

This book is part of the Prize given to
the winner of the poetry contest.

For more information and to see our
growing catalog of choices, please go to
www.lummoxpress.com

www.ingramcontent.com/pod-product-compliance
Lightning Source LLC
Chambersburg PA
CBHW051719040426
42446CB00008B/969